THE ESOTERIAN

THE ESOTERIAN

RAMBLINGS OF A MADMAN

A COLLECTION OF POEMS BY

EHMBEE WAY

I'm no longer afraid to fail; failure is nothing more than experience gained through earnest experimentation. What truly terrifies me is the comforting numbness of a life without purpose. For I would rather die, as a failure, chasing my dreams, than to stagnate in complacency, living forever without them.

For Penny
You spoke without words. You loved without doubt.

TABLE OF CONTENTS

INTRODUCTION

What's in a Name?

*T*he *Esoterian: Ramblings of a Madman* is a collection of poems I wrote (mostly) between April and September of 2022. Among other topics, these poems address death, spirituality, mind control, love, purpose, regret, maturation, mental illness and the inescapable grasp of time. At least, that's how *I* would describe them. To others, however, a good number of these poems probably seem like nonsensical, esoteric ramblings.

And while it's true that I *could* attempt to demystify some of this aforementioned ambiguity, in order to try and make everything a bit more *exo*teric—more obvious in meaning and more encompassing for the masses—doing so would, undoubtedly, feel like a betrayal of the self. That's probably because, in life, and in art especially, I've always placed a high sense of value on free thinking and other non-conformist traits. Additionally, I'm a fervent believer in the subjectivity of art and in the theory that an author's intent needn't shape a reader's interpretation. And if this premise is true, what, then, would be the point in amending this admittedly imperfect but also notably honest collection? Self-reflection—the cornerstone of poetry—is, after all, impossible without honesty.

So, as the title of my collection might suggest, I've decided to lean into my esoteric poetry—to "call it for what it is," as my old boss used to say. After all, at this point in life, I'm old enough to know that it's a lot easier, healthier and more natural to be true to my work than it is to try and change it to please others.

Thanks for reading and I hope you enjoy!

Sincerely,

Ehmbee Way

A RELUCTANT CHAUFFEUR

She's lost in between worlds—
her minted name still pressed into my miserable heart.

She'll return it erelong—
melted and useless, in this place she'll not stay.

She's an unanswered prayer—
one I'll soon release, to await me again.

She's two pleading, brown eyes—
peering beyond my murderous intent.

She's a welcoming lamb—
loyal and ready for that which she's craved.

She's prostrate and listless—
trembling bravely, behind her reluctant chauffer.

She's a teary contradiction—
impelling, somehow, that I both hurry and dawdle.

She's bound for that room—
where my irrevocable decision insidiously looms.

She's a poisonous sponge—
surrounding my soul 'til I follow her home.

MODERN AMISH

Technological waves crash against the stubborn Modern Amish.

They try and fling him from his two-hundred horses.

Rusted and fuming, the aging steed balks with rubber hooves in the street.

A persistent ocean of electric life—algorithms designed to erode his world.

From every direction, it bombards him with salty figures and nefarious codes.

Afraid of drowning, he secures his handheld preserver.

(A mini-ocean in and of itself), it pushes him forward, while he idles and his sneakers dig in.

He's now enveloped by a promise of ease that would just as soon drown him.

Sink or swim; he's a slave to its will.

Swallowing cities and countries. People and time.

For forty days, it reigns. Zeros and ones splashing onto the brim of his fitted hat.

We'll all be consumed by its treacherous depths.

Across from the Modern, buggies clop carelessly, through puddles of stats.

Bearded and defiant carpenters; they've learned to pause time.

So the Would-Be watches, scoffing with hypocritical admiration.

Thousand-eyed cameras with perfect memory—they log the scene.
Fueled by our vanity, they stoke their advance toward our
   inevitable end.
For boiling seas heed neither his pause nor mine.

We'll all burn just the same.

MY COMFY BOX

My comfy box… It displaces the truth.
I noticed, yesterday, that his did so too.

Mine a bit larger, in a field that's been cut.
His with a lid I'd rather not shut.

Mine above and his below,
Both of them soon, in similar rows.

They stack us together—a difference in time.
Yet one that will fade (my quiet opine).

With similar price-tags and pillows and galore,
Mine in plain sight and his nevermore.

I feel microscopic, in my box under stars.
While his stay attached (engraved in his arms).

A plethora of comforts I cannot deny.
Yet still we're encased, like the liquor we'd buy.

Too soon to leave but too late to stay.
In two different boxes, we feel the same way.

Our comfy boxes: in separate spaces they ration.
Aided by time, in receding the chasm.

SHE HUNTS

She's on the hunt again. Old bones creaking like the floorboards she's annexed. Shrewd yellowy eyes narrowing. Invading her prospect's periphery, with a deliberate and lascivious gaze.

She hunts with a saunter. Choosy and slow (the cunning and beguiling predator). Unconcerned—the Nimble Naïve dart about, trying to nab a bite. Careless. Reckless. Impetuous. They are flies for the fruit. The seasoned carnivore's indifference—flashed in a subtle grin.

She hunts to augment. A den for her pups and her pups' pups. She can taste it in the poison that drips from her milky-white fangs. Acid splashing on high-trafficked tile.

She hunts from the past. Gnarled incisors smoothed like pearls. Her coat: grizzled but rewoven. Her claws: caked with paint. They scrape and scathe. Each step: a spritz of lime on a hot grill. She's closing the distance.

She hunts for purpose. Ego. Assurance. She's a relic made newer with every kill. Rejuvenated. Plasticized: his card to her body. A hallucination in the eyes of her prey. The wily wolf: she's spotted… so she makes her move.

THE JINN

They built it a temple and invited it in.
They built it to trap the ubiquitous Jinn.

They want it to answer their wildest dreams.
They wanted to fit it inside of their schemes.

So they make up their rules and lecture to me.
And forgo their freedom, just to be free.

There's this rule and that rule and that rule and this…
"And you better not falter:" this warning, they hiss.

They think it's exclusive: their walls and their rules.
Their shepherds: exhausted (from herding such mules).

They transformed from sheep and they think it's divine.
They think it's because of the Jinn in their shrine.

They think it's still there and, sadly, they're right.
It's *every*where—both in darkness and light.

It will not be captured. Its will is its own.
It's present here… across seas… and at home.

It left them a note, which they twist and distort,
wishing their rules, are what I'd support.

Its message as simple as flight to a dove:
Just love, believe and always put you above.

From this they get war, judgement and hate.
But lucky for them: it's never too late.

And so I observe their cathedral-like trap,
climbing their tree, while avoiding the sap.

Across from my branch: its window—it's open.
And the Jinn—it's still there (just as we were hoping).

INTO THE WELL

Your prediction postponed.

> Where propaganda, unrest and tyranny became musical televisions, MS-DOS and a proclivity for denim. Where my big brother stalks only department stores. Where your aptly-named nightmare was coined.

> But still looms nonetheless.

Your farm, a fiction.

> Where four legs became two. Where a cunning sacrifice led to a deceptive adhesion. Where our privilege became our chains.

> Still truer every day.

Your words, enduring.

> Where the residue of entertainment dissolves aged alarms. Where classrooms miss ominous ink. Where I read, while I can.

> 'Til you're lost, burned and banned.

MY FLESHY MACHINE

This fleshy machine,
has no guarantee.
Just some vague expectations I've yet to redeem.

It could bring me luck.
It might just get stuck
but sooner or later, they'll all run amuck.

This one exploded.
That one's corroded
and I often feel like mine's overloaded.

So, with endless revisions
and countless conditions,
I've given consent: automatic decisions.

I pay it no mind—
these urges of mine.
They exist in the programs to which they're assigned.

Yes, it rests when it needs;
when empty, it feeds.
Though, when inconvenient, I do intercede.

It can maneuver:
this "Hurdle diffuser."
While I endlessly ponder on ways to improve her.

But when I reflect,
on all my neglect,
it's too overwhelming for me to dissect.

Yet still I proclaim:
No one can I blame,
when I'm forced to return it, to back whence it came.

WAITING

A consuming terror.
Where consciousness persists.
And the flesh finally fails.
It's always looming.
And I'm waiting.

The chilling clarity.
The impending inevitability.
The world's indifference:
Perfunctory, mechanical, ominous.
And I'm waiting.

On the living room floor.
Phone just out of reach.
Water glugging, from out of its plastic receptacle.
I can feel the dampening carpet.
And I'm waiting.

Secured to the table.
The frantic words of strangers resounding in my perfect ears.
My eyes—distant and unresponsive.
But I can still see them.
And I'm waiting.

Sprawled out against the sidewalk.
Its gritty embrace—like cool sandpaper on my face.
While the warm ichor seeps out from within me.

Metallic and bitter, in the back of my useless throat.
And I'm waiting.

Alone.
Secluded and forgotten.
These twisted and distorted memories only perplex.
This empty room—it's full of strangers.
And I'm waiting.

For those few terrifying seconds, which have lasted for most of my life.

THE BOUNDLESS BLUE

I let go…

Of my self-doubting sermons
Of my rationalized fear
Of trepidation, excuses and caution and care

I let go…

Of my animal instincts
Of advisements decreed
Of their warnings, their anger, their bargains, their pleas

I let go…

Of her hand clasped in mine
Of her billion-year pull
Of the rickety old beam, cutting wind like a tool

I let go…

Of those fast-shrinking wings
Of imposing thin lines
Of my rank, as I sink toward the plots they divide

I let go…

Of my home and its pull
Of myself and my time
Of my nature, my being, my intended design

I let go…

And found a moment of bliss
And moved through the mist
And, as the ground reached for me, I wondered, "What if?"

I let go

THE DEMON INSIDE

Padding inside a reflective, gray jacket. Blue jeans. Haggard boots. Fingerless gloves, pulled over vampiric-white hands. Dark sunglasses inside flip-visored, open-faced fiberglass.

He's stirring. Welling inside of me, as I don the uniform.

My greasy steed: dirty-white and death-splattered. European. Nimble. Light. Smeared and unkempt. Glistening anyway.

His possession looming. A contagious smile spreading across my face like a pox.

The plot: southbound. Where time has no grasp. Where the working beasts dwell—saddled by a misplaced century (where I'm the anachronism). Where winding turns and open fields form a welcoming desolation. Where blue-hairs, plows and road-apples abound. Where counterfeit training-wheelers pretend. Where we all scamper, under a sparsely-clouded blue.

His demonic drool, dripping down the back of my throat. Warm and addicting. Anticipating my solitary escape (where my risk is my own). His only way out. I won't gamble with hers.

Sending the vertical stand horizontal and flush. Squeezing: metal to rubber. Driving: toes toward the ground. Lurching forward. I'm on so I'm off. Through invisible yellows, past fashionable pirates on parade. Flicking my wrist; searching for twists. Winged pests crash like hurled rocks, while I salute the northbound (imposters and cohorts alike). Blustering winds reverberate. Drowning me out of myself. Carving my presence into a dark, endless embrace. I am free and yet…

He has me.

RUT

There' s a rut in the road,
though it's covered with snow.

Waiting there, underneath
those icy white sheets.

It's inconveniently placed,
yet I cross it with haste.

Cuz this wintry mix
is coming down quick.

* * *

Try alternate courses?
I've barely the horses.

So I'm jostled inside
my incommodious ride.

But I know that one day
we'll spring from this gray.

And so I trudge along,
just humming my song.

* * *

There's a rut in the road,
where the sunflowers grow.

It's right there between
the asphalt and green.

Still inconveniently placed,
in the road its defaced.

But I pay it no mind,
coasting down the incline

*   *   *

They must fill it in soon—
those orange-vested goons.

They'd be otherwise odd,
since the blizzard's now thawed.

So I wait for the city,
(a new bruise on my kidney).

While trudging along,
with my suff'ring prolonged.

*   *   *

There's a rut in the road,
by a field, freshly mowed.

But with my motorcycle,
it's barely a trifle.

I approach with discretion,
from my two-wheeled invention.

And dodge with such ease
whizzing by, as I please.

*   *   *

But sometimes I forget
and am met with regret.

When I lift from my seat,
in the stark summer heat.

The rut's still in my way,
on this road where I play.

Yet, I still trudge along,
whether right, whether wrong.

*   *   *

There's a rut in the road,
over which leaves have blown.

Bright yellows and greens
when the fall intervenes.

I could find a new way
but then what would that say?

'Bout this rhythm I'm in
(places I've never been).

*   *   *

So with windows rolled up,
I still bounce in my truck.

A comfortable nuisance.
An uncomfortable prudence.

And the rut—it persists
so my conscience insists…

That I just trudge along,
as I've done all year long.

    *   *   *

AND YET I STRUGGLE

Striving for validation; dying for purpose; reaching for more…
To want improvement: such is the burden of selfishness.
And yet I want…

Reconsidering; reexamining; reevaluating; revising…
To endlessly question: such is the anguish of indecision.
And yet I question…

Yearning for adulation; aching for touch; thirsting for passion…
To long for the flesh: such is the cunning deception of lust.
And yet I long…

Discrediting castigations; disparaging diatribes; belittling
   conclusions…
To silence my reprisal: such is the indefensibility of reticence.
And yet I hold my tongue…

Hunger; shelter; wealth; ineptitude; disease; destruction; death…
To worry over that which I am helpless: such is curse of anxiety.
And yet I worry.

Perseverance; acceptance; restraint; forgiveness; faith…
To struggle for good: such is the cornerstone of rebirth.
And yet I struggle…

JOANNE

A cursed city, under picturesque, western skies.
(where rotten souls fester under an inviting heat lamp).

Poseidon's mist tunneling through two smudgy glass drawbridges—
a rousing revival for the displaced bohemian below.

Joanne: a relocated foreigner (their heartland to hers).
So her yawn curls the corners inside this cramped and open life.

Her metal door roaring along its track (gliding effortlessly,
    while she tugs).
Sandy asphalt greets dirty feet, as she flows toward a concrete hut.

An outdoor shower chain, hung from the sky. Salty water and
    door-less stalls.
Identical choices line the sultry, gritty hut, where she drips free of
    false rain.

Disapproving eyes under shielded lenses—they watch her
    saunter home.
There, she'll trap them on canvass—foul grimace and all.

Pastels and psychedelic swirls augment their dreary dispositions,
while a cool ocean breeze spatters the scene and adds a flair
    of its own.

High heels and glossy loafers stifle the passing crowd, as they watch
    her forge life.
Rats in a maze. Their expensive cheeses—both toxic and unimaginative.

They scurry to amass as much as they can—
eagerly trained by bland and invisible gods.

She'll eat from a bin. Stuffed and belching up paints that sustain her.
Still… scoffing vermin comb their tangled fur in confusion and
    sanctimonious pity.

Their muffled whispers gaining strength with distance:
"Isolated. Deluded. A broke dilettante," they assure themselves.

Even so… they all wonder.
They all secretly wonder…

How could one live in such unnatural ways?
So their eyes ask the question, as they lock on the street.

SMUDGE

This smudge—it's a nuisance.
>A persistent and enduring blemish.
>Distorting the subject I still behold.

This surface—it's marred.
>A traitorous landscape of lies.
>Blending fiction and fact, as I scrub.

This method—it's useless.
>An ineffective and futile task.
>Straining body and spirit alike.

This reflection—it's compromised.
>A flawed and disappointing imitation.
>Mocking and rejecting my vain adulation.

This smudge—it's prevailing.
>An irremovable, rotting perversion.
>Imprisoning me, forever, in the moment.

ECHO

On a ledge by her window:
a decorative blue tin.
It waits there in limbo,
for her life to begin.

By cracked glass, it exists—
a calling-card uncreated.
'Neath a bird who persists,
by reflectors serrated.

Its rain-enhanced luster,
its brightness, its sheen.
Above it they cluster,
both craving caffeine.

A splish-splashy landing;
doves perched there to stare.
By crinkled blue branding,
this ledge, they both share.

Not far from a mirror,
with a luminous dazzle.
In a room with cheap beer,
and a young girl who's frazzled.

They think it unfair—
this girl's dark reflection.
They'd make quite the pair,
could they agree on direction.

They're wiser than she,
yet still just an echo.
They're happy and free;
she's not quite yet there though.

For lascivious hounds,
she primps to prepare.
While feathers abound,
and she tussles her hair.

She's caking on rouge
when the fowl eye their treasure.
And her deficit looms,
in a life without pleasure.

Her lipstick's depleted;
she stalls for more time.
The doves have retreated
to the back to her mind.

Another counts money.
She's watching with shame.
"Good job out there, Honey."
They've *both* been renamed.

The drunken, old bard—
he's in charge of rebranding.
Her name's on his card;
it's okay, notwithstanding.

"It's echo," he bellows,
through smoke-yellowed speakers.
He's an opportunist,
encircled by tweakers.

Her astral-beaked gazer,
across a short chasm—
knows it stings like a taser
(his words make her spasm).

"You'll love her," he cries—
"This one is perfecto!"
Her anxiety grips her,
when he says, "Welcome Echo!"

The name—it's not hers,
but she took it sans-protest:
surrounded by curs,
and an uneasy hostess.

She takes a deep breath
and heads for the stage.
It feels like her death,
but she tempers her rage.

A wobbly summit…
Zombies claw at her heel.
They want her to plummet—
to proposition a deal.

Listlessly staring,
at a window outside…
Two doves form a paring,
while the patrons imbibe.

They're wiser than she,
yet still just an echo.
They're happy and free;
she's not quite yet there though.

With wrapper in claw,
they ascend toward the clouds.
Her heart, they'll soon thaw.
On this much, she vows.

She'll find doves of her own:
both crinkled and blue.
With her echo dethroned,
and encased there for you.

THE FACELESS

We are the faceless collective.
Systematized, hollow golems.
Senseless husks you peruse at your leisure.

We are the numeric phalanx.
Dismantled and inventoried.
Arranged for invisible suitors.

We are the vacuous brood.
Our very essence, a toxic contamination.
Drained from the holes in our chests.

We are the subhuman horde.
Probed by merciless and fickle judges.
To quietly serve 'neath their ominous shadows.

We are clumps of soulless clay.
Imperfect and plentiful.
To squish and remold at your whimsy.

We're the innumerable blind.
'Til we unstitch our eyes
And leave you behind.

IN THE SOMEWHERE

A surprise gathering, in a minimalistic hall. Early June. Chairs. Carpet. Decorative collages (esoteric and transitory). A suit he's been wearing for days. It's soaking up the T-shirts and tattoos. No sweat. Not a single wrinkle. The makeup: tasteful. Hands folded, expectantly. Ready to absorb my concern.

Reticent—this good-natured firebrand. His closed eyes fixed on me. Waiting. Can't talk. Not here. The others: distracted. So I close my eyes and liven him up.

We're back in his car. Malt liquor. Asphalt craters and faded white lines. A greasy spoon behind us. "Screaming infidelities." Surfeit drinking. Smiles on our lips. Same questions. Same answers. I cock my neck. The ceiling: bluish upholstery (yellowed, with our toxic breath). A big swig and I wince. Then he's gone. His Confessional too. Silence… 'til I hear him through the speakers…

No "voice…" But… it's him. A disc skipping like May seniors. I eject him but he's still beating. From The Somewhere. This disconnected reflection… Silent. Flat. Round. Inside: the old man who killed me. Our eyes lock and my drink sours. I've forgotten how to talk… how to think.

A thinly-concentrated beam of rainbow slicing through reality when I flick my wrist. It catches the sky, like a fishing line in a tree. Twisting. Pulling. Tension. Then… the ensuing whirlpool. Violently yanking existence into the circular drain, in the middle of the tiny makeshift mirror.

It's a brief moment that lasts for eternity. In the void of The Somewhere. Nothing but his communicative reverberations. He's bouncing off of my bones. The newest transmission that's older than time. Incomprehensible in my state. But… I muse…

A final white flash and I'm back. The suit too. Odd, yes, but even with my own. So I accept it. And this new, old man hobbles home. That cadence… gregarious and relentless. Near but unattainable. Trapped inside an antiquated medium, where I live. So I wait… until I hear it again.

TURN

A perpetual game of Russian Roulette.
I pass to my neighbors, my family, my friends.

We pass 'round the world; we pass to coworkers.
To doctors, to teachers, to bright-eyed, young servers.

We pass to the young; we pass to the old.
We all take our turns; we all must enroll.

So everyone plays yet no one can win.
Just holding our breath, while the steel chamber spins.

And some rounds are lead but others are not.
And not all are quick from the cannon they're shot.

Some take their time, circling our heads.
But sooner or later, that's where they'll embed.

Our insidious gamble; our constant concern.
Though none can withdraw so we all take our turn.

THE DARKENING WIND

It always finds its way in—
this treacherous wind.

Snuffer of flames.
Taker of names.

Another cyclone foretold.
Another candle blown cold.

So the light here, it fades,
like a passing parade.

And my eyes strain to see
(glimpse what's coming for me).

And my ears catch its howl,
intermittent and foul.

And it wafts through my nose,
causing me to suppose,

That it carried her scent—
her quiet lament.

Dead flowers and pine.
Always theirs ('til they're mine).

Whether breeze, whether gust,
swirling always amongst…

Ashes and candles,
on dust-covered mantles.

'Bove a cold fireplace,
with no blaze; with no trace.

On extant candles it clings—
These wax furnishings.

In a room, colder now,
where I'm forced to avow.

That I still sense the smoke—
that shapeless, gray rogue.

Dancing against
a whirlwind commenced.

And these flames fading fast,
'round these wicks, which won't last.

Lights constantly thinned,
by this darkening wind.

SONG OF THE FIREFLY

With a flash, you danced your way through my head.
>You couldn't stay long.
>It's not where you belong.

This illuminating reflection (like my secretive pond).
>You never knew
>how I kept it for you.

Drained, now, and barren—a pit I fill with myself.
>We could have met there.
>Red, in my wet hair.

With similar flickers—electric flutters on wind.
>But it's hard to remember,
>with this hole in the center.

'Til we unite in their fire that's been burning since time.
>Lemon embers so plenty
>(all wafting here gently).

Where perpetual billions buzz a fiery sky.
>They speak without sound
>and their message astounds.

Telepathically one (with each essence preserved).
>They're talking but how?
>Never knew until now.

In an instant I have every flash in the land.
>> You'll have them too…
>> They're stored here for you.

Simultaneous comprehension; harmonious swarm
>> For all fireflies
>> (all that have died).

Completely fulfilled, now. Governed by love.
>> No misunderstanding
>> (their flashes enchanting).

But you aren't ready so I'll wait in the glow.
>> From this hole in the ground,
>> where these flies gather 'round.

UNRAVELED

Their heads abutting.
His eyes: swimming toward the falling sun.
Hers: Eastbound.
His: scratchy and dead.
Hers: scrolling.

Their futures conflicting.
His: uprooted.
Hers: freshly sown.
His: pointless.
Hers: the point.

Their embrace: uncertain.
His: surrendered; defeated.
Hers: enigmatic.
His: withdrawn and limp.
Hers: disengaging.

Their goodbye: disingenuous.
His: a lament.
Hers: an inconvenient formality.

Their march: separate.
His: a despondent shuffle.
Hers: an inspired jaunt.

Their fates: unraveled,
in perfect, perpetual, inequitable unity.

ENTOMBED

Sirens stinging my eyes, as my mind implodes in on itself.
Fate closing the distance, as the sky walls me in.
My heart—it's gagging on life turned to curdled sludge.

I am undone.
And I am doomed.

Drowning beneath steamy asphalt, as its current drags me below
    the waves.
Her hand evaporating like steam, as she reaches in unseen.
The sun—it's lunging toward us, while red and blue specters converge.

Nowhere to run.
And I am consumed.

Tar filling my lungs, as I sink toward a molten core.
Sweat pouring from my soul, as the holstered judge approaches.
Despair—its odor masked by metallic oils, powders and lead.

This is the one.
And I am entombed.

BURNED AT THE STAKE

They warned me about you…
You are the shaman they slander—
the fangless monster, hiding under my bed.

They've found another place for you.
And so your presence fills the threatening pyre,
hanging like a haze—cloaked in a sweet, invisible stink.

I breathed you into my secret smile.
Picking you like a guitar and trading in their slow, chemicalized death.
You're pure as the forest rain tickling the canopy.

They tell me you're no good for me.
Belching their nonsensical pronouncements, from north-facing,
    linear stools,
(swaying wife-beaters, vandalizers and manslaughterers alike).

Scandalized at the stake; they bluff with torches that dare not
    touch you.
You're the sticky, double-edged blade cutting through their illusion—
impartially dispelling the miasma around even my own consciousness.

With spirited breath, they scoff at such miracles.
You are the subject of their ridicule.
But you keep me as I am, while the unrestrained mob slurs their
    every impulse.

They've found you guilty, Oh Treacherous Healer.
You're the thousand-year-old, red-haired counselor in the forest,
where you swung open a large, agrestal doorway to introspection
    and epiphany.

So I swipe a torch and ignite you myself.
Like the prophets of Nebuchadnezzar, you burn without fussing,
releasing your jumbled musings through the smoke.

As they flee, your ashes swirl and form a blueprint in the sky.
Both my thoughts and his, churn inside my skull,
relaxing me and bringing me closer… 'til we kill you again.

CHASING THE LIGHT

My heart has grown stale so I soak it with ale.
This place is a corpse-breeding crypt.
To my right is a light that would burn through the night
but it's much too bright for my grip.

It should shine for me, but It doesn't, you see.
So I try to stand out from the dead.
My attempts are in vain and it causes me pain,
for without it, this will be my end.

I'd pour out my guts and watch them stick in the ruts,
as they plopped and I puked on the floor.
The rusty incision would make Death's decision—
one that my life could no longer endure.

You'd simply give me a smile, with my guts in a pile
and they'd take me away in a hearse.
But die as I might, without you, my light,
the pain could not be much worse.

I'd scoop out my eyes and assume a new guise.
With a blindfold, I'd crawl on the floor.
They'd squish in my hands, like hot melted sand.
For you, I would do this and more.

You'd say something trite about the loss of my sight
and they'd take me away to learn Braille.
I'd fail to see, your light around me,
so this life would seem pointless and frail.

I'd stick my legs in a fan—become half a man.
Blood would spray throughout the whole tomb.
Severed in twain, in shock and in pain,
I'd die from this new mortal wound.

Never to walk by your side, legless, I died
and they threw me somewhere in a grave.
I'd scratch and I'd pound—never making a sound.
I'd do this—for your light I crave.

My attempts would all fail and my heart would impale
itself on fence post for you.
So try as I might, I'm surrounded by night.
But with your light, it's all nothing new.

COOKEDBOOKS

- Begin by coating a medium-sized corporation with a liberal spritzing of nepotism and then simmer for twenty years.

- In a separate area, combine equal-parts servings of customer gullibility, spurious marketing claims and one finely-aged celebrity endorsement.

- Stir mixture together until its aroma begins to resemble excrement from a bull.

- Dump "bull concoction" into the simmering, medium-sized corporation.

- While waiting for everything to sizzle, begin baking an underqualified manufacturer at constantly changing temperatures that are impossible to track. Make sure to sprinkle plenty of "back-alley" deals and disorganization into the mix, while doing so.

- After another five years, dump the deep-baked manufacturer into the sizzling corporation and push buttons wildly, while attempting to set a temperature and time.

- Add a steamed medley of greed, plenty of markup and several disconnected egomaniacs for flavor.

- Season with a dash of fraud and slather with snake oil before serving.

THE WICCAN

She's hanging puppets from a noose.
A cutlery drawer emptied into his already lifeless form.

Yearning to switch his place with hers, she recalls the pact:
"Betrayed but forgiven;" though she regrets her consent.

So she quakes beneath her medieval warning—
her unease manifested in smoky chains of rage and uncorked despair.

The Wiccan. Invoking a curse from the Earth.
A deaf god beneath concrete, glass-piles and so many butts…

They're scattered between the witch and her beau (or Jncos and an
    oily floor).
The remnants of mute therapists she's burned while she waits.

She's waiting on her golem—his now-hardened clay, still warm from
    her touch…
Summoned by emergency logos exploding inside his high-tech tether.

So she stares one-eyed daggers, while the other wanders wistfully
(paganized and tuned to a world he still cannot see).

It's her insightful corruption—her beautiful bane.
These idolatrous dualities infecting her brain.

They've cloaked him in shadowy goo (her strength now her curse).
Neither a devilish monster nor terrestrial saint, he laments…

What only he can see.

CHARISMATIC DETOURS

A sense of enlightenment.
Just give them your mind.
A doctrine of lies,
from recycled divined.

A utopia rising,
on the backs of its horde.
The happiest slaves,
all welcomed aboard.

A quest built on purpose
(Charismatic detours).
Stockholm-ing concessions:
they've become connoisseurs.

Unity: paramount.
Conformity: key.
Give them your all
and they'll let you be free.

Comradery-driven.
Lost family and friends.
The old become new,
when you've made their amends.

Simplistic living.
Unencumbered and broke.
Possession-less mob.
He feasts while they choke.

To belong, love and work.
Contributions distorted.
The best of intentions,
abused and contorted.

RAIN-DANCE

Alone, he approaches the barren, linoleum wasteland,
under the uninspired, auditory template blanketing the room.
Beneath its covers, the crowd snickers like a candy bar.
Their low, anticipatory murmur—as slick as the painted lines in
    the road, after a good rain.

Through the translucent covers: the approaching grays loom large.
Bereft of hydration, these desert nomads curse the concept.
A unanimous thirst that he alone can feel,
as he steps between strobing, manufactured rainbows.

That waterless puddle… It sticks to his shoe.
He doesn't need it.
No faux courage to fuel his decision.
This, he does soaking dry.

His undulating body fails to sync with his mind.
His eyes and ears disgust him.
His throat is dry and his breath is clean.
They hate him for it.

Spirit-cleansed, he's lost that old inspiration.
Still… they abound aplenty and whisper in his ear:
"We can help."
Unimpressed, he's up for getting down, under the cloud.

His unique gyrations inspire the herd.
A few thirsty sheilas clop onto the elevated plains and encircle him.
He can't give them what they want.
These powerless succubuses—they try and nuzzle but he pays them
    no heed.

Surrounded by spirits and cattle, he's had enough.
His rain-dance failed the past but invigorates the moment.
Enthralled with their gathering reflections, he slips by unnoticed,
as they whoop and holler in choreographed debauchery.

As he mounts his mechanical steed, a thunderous bolt ignites the sky.
He's washed dry, as he races home, in the storm no one wants.

HUNTING HEADS

I'll cut off your head, to grant you new life.
Affix it with glee, to the tip of my pike.

Tasked from afar, while I sharpen my blade.
Hunting and stalking—my gruesome new trade.

My victims impress me; the average distress me.
For only the right skull will earn me a blood fee.

"It cannot be this. It cannot be that.
"It cannot be booming or fledgling or fat."

Discriminate tastes from our set benefactor.
Skirting the law—our tribe of recanters.

They say, "Lure them in. Promise the heavens."
And if we discard them, grow deaf to their questions."

"They'll fetch us no silver so waste not your time.
"Concentrate, only, on what you must find."

The neck of affluents—that's where I will carve.
We could raise the poor but we just let them starve.

There's no profit in that. Our task is specific.
No ethics or laws shall become our staunch critic.

I'll behead a count and then make him a duke.
"But peasants die peasants, earning only rebuke."

Commissioned by death to decapitate.
And offering my neck so he'll reciprocate.

GRIP

A cloud of carcinogens and she's gone
(she's absconded through the smoky mirage).
In its dissipation, her absence stings just the same.

She's truncated, in the lingering remnants of her toxic haze.
A disembodied hand still clutching his wrist.
He's failed to unhook the rigor mortis-like insistence of its infectious
    fingers.

Her grip: enduring and ubiquitous.
In the toolshed, he's undertaken the task of removing it,
with sweat splashing onto useless, steel-bladed-instruments.

Invoking the modern shaman—a ritualistic type of relief.
Pills and potables—they immobilize his will but not the
    permanence of his insight.
Their collective quacking: unable to sever the bond…

Her greening flesh is rotting, under the frigid summer heat.
That zombified hand still clinging and digging. Deeper. Always
    deeper.
Its putrid aroma never far from his thoughts…

For years, it prevails: inert and parasitic.
Like an engorged tick he cannot reach, it's a part of him.
He's accepted his disease but he'll not succumb to it.

In perpetuity, they exist: host and hand.
'Til he awakens to a curious, dusty, fleshless appendage.
Brittled through time, then, her dusty bones effortlessly snap, under
the grit of his fortified grip.

YOU'RE LIFE

Like a barrage of pummeling fists,
bathed in the blood you cannot resist.
Your beating…

Like the cells you use to cage me—
facing truth: that they sustain me.
You're the key…

Like the chamber you fill with silvery rounds,
And the other you don't, where my life is yet bound.
Your control…

Like a syringe spraying doubt in my cell
(to pump it back out; there's a rig and a well).
Your directing…

Like the attack you perpetrated—
Aquarius lore—so celebrated.
You're the source…

Until the day…
I'm forced to leave you.

DISTILLED DWELLING

In my aluminum cave,
where I hide from the day
and the stresses of life—such an endless charade.

This rectangular den…
where I'm prone to pretend
that I am at ease and that I have found Zen.

It's my dwelling on blocks,
where I'll often remark
"I am chasing a dream (or a dark paradox)."

Cuz my single-wide shack
sits still on its track,
while moving me forward—while yanking me back.

See: this decorative shed,
where I fashioned my bed
keeps the world at bay… out of reach… overhead.

While this portable cell,
(half-Heaven, half-Hell)
Recycles my doubt (such a strange parallel).

And my fragile-shelled home,
where I sit all alone,
distills my existence into this tiny poem.

PLAN B

I'm her aptly-named contraceptive,
absorbed and dismantled, 'til I'm a speck of myself.

My lingering sinew forming walls 'round her heart.
Enclosed, now, and vacant, I protect from outside.

She's taken me fully.
So I encircle her soul.

It's a whirlpool that rips me apart.
Each piece—a new brick for a wall never done.

Inside and out, more consumed with each dose.
"The diluted placeholder on guard."

A tolerable leper, leaving pieces for scrap.
Collected and piled 'til she's ready to try.

Then she flushes me out, though I remain in her blood
(disintegrating, there, with no plan of my own).

REBORN WITH SAINT PATRICK

For decades, I lived inside echoes of your glory. Emaciated and wistful. Nibbling crumbs of nostalgia—bitter with age. This incurable habit: a morose, stale shuffle.

I left you suspended in stasis—an auditory ghost amassing secret caches, while lesser stewards pick at your scraps. Industrious frauds bending cords, charts and will. Dancing on graves that must have been yours. So I carved out my ears and put the scraps in a pod.

Then you rose! Your restorative call ringing out through the ether. Fixing me. Beckoning me. Grabbing, shaking, filling me! Our triumvirate merger: the comatose, vibrant and me! A reborn archeologist rips through my cocoon so I search.

Harmonious exploration. Gems carelessly missed. Your words serenade my euphonious discovery. Measured and timed. Scaled and patterned. They tickle my budding ears as they grow anew in your presence.

My confidant; my counselor; my partner; my muse. Reborn in The Falls. Amongst drunken leprechauns, green tights and your crowd-pleasing shanties. You persist. You were missed.

THE RIOTOUS WHITE SEA

Drowning in a placid, white sea.
No waves, no clouds, no life.
Just the neon glow accosting me.
No moon, no stars, no tide.

Treading space in the abyss…
I reach out in search of a line.
But the colorless sea—she's my mistress
and she's dragging me under the brine.

Floundering here, no preserver in sight.
Only mermaids who offer no help.
Their nonsensical shanties: more like a blight
(sung from their homes, in the kelp).

I yet hear their chatter, from under the water
(sounds of every variety).
Still, this is the course that I must now charter
(alone and removed from society).

Cutting white gulfs with invisible hosts—
their babble is filling the deep.
If only I could, I'd silence these ghosts
and then I'd hear nary a peep.

Wanting to leave, I grip at my keys—
a weapon to aid my escape.
Can they lead me to peace? Can they drain these white seas
and silence this audial rape?

And though I can't stand them, there's no end to these fathoms
(leaving my mind quite destroyed).
So, under duress, I'm able to manage
to float here amongst the great void.

But the howling persists, as I stroke at the white
(still holding so tight to my keys).
They're the muse I'll invoke though the night,
as I swim to wherever I please.

CHARGE

The grizzled buck and his disinterested progeny:
lusting for freedom; fenced into a property.

Butting heads in a field, where the two make their home.
The young still dependent but longing to roam.

He won't learn to forage, to fight or to hunt.
He wants only to gallop, to feast and pull stunts.

So the two square up and charge each other again.
Cracking heads when they wake; cracking heads 'til they bed.

It's this way for years. It's a site to behold.
Charging at will, 'til a change did unfold.

It began when the pup learned to dart through the trees,
tripping and stumbling and buckling his knees.

So the buck showed his son how to dodge with such ease,
and together they'd run wherever they pleased.

But it didn't last long and the stag disappeared.
His progeny, though, had yet persevered.

And when it was done, so little was said.
They'd spent most of their lives just butting their heads.

HOLDING ON

I'm holding on,
though my heart has grown weak.
I'm holding on,
though the future seems bleak.

I'm holding on,
mooshy, withered, old hands.
I'm holding on,
mooshy, quickening sands.

I'm holding on,
with the fast-melting snow.
I'm holding on,
with a mind to let go.

I'm holding on,
while my grip starts to fade.
I'm holding on,
while there's no need to stay.

I'm holding on,
but my fall should be nigh.
I'm holding on,
but I still don't know why.

I'm holding on.

SATURATED BEASTS

Disguised by steamy waves of heat: a filthy mirage beyond the clearing.
They feverishly scamper toward it—the tethers of their servitude
    dragging behind them…

Willfully rebellious—paying no heed to the frustrated cries
    behind them,
they fully commit to their transgression.

Submission be damned. Repercussions too.
They're overwhelmed with the allure of a natural and simplistic bliss.

As the distance between us grows, I'm forced to confront their
    innate superiority.
They unconsciously demonstrate it with raw speed and easily-adaptable,
    self-sufficient constitutions.

And so they shed the constraints of our expectations—to flirt with
    wild, unencumbered freedom.
They'll heed no instruction today.

Wallowing down, in the grimy Earth (where that suspected mirage
    proves true),
they've enthusiastically abandoned the shackles of proper decorum.

The natural pull of playful freedom—too enticing to be subverted
    with domestication.
They saturate their otherwise pristine coats (unrepentant and
    utterly flummoxed as to my seemingly incomprehensible
    decision to remain stationary).

CULMINATION POINT

Victim or victor.
Thousands of needling eyes pierce my back as I approach my fickle fate.

Risk or protect.
I've the clothes on my back, an indeterminate curse and this
    clacking handful of chips.

Omens or chance.
Destitution looming over the chaos of indecipherable ambiguities.

Win or lose.
My trembling fingers fumble futures and fungible plastics.

To be or to not.
This mission, this partner, this gamble, this life.

Red or black.
I'd throw them both to prolong my distress.

Earth or fire.
Similar ending slabs where rigor mortis clutches cursed tokens.

To you, I defer.
So my curse can endure.

WE MARCH

Whether by…

The heedless misguided:
    [Cold arms for twisted minds.]
    [Dark agendas gathering mass.]
    [Radioactive mushrooms towering like Babel.]

Or the nihilist's creed:
    [Malnourished and grotesque.]
    [Imbibing on poisons.]
    [Poised for the ultimate surrender.]

Or Gaia's fickle nature:
    [Vindictive, pitiless and reductive.]
    [Gathering force from within.]
    [Spinning and taunting rocks that just miss.]

Or this finite design:
    [Malfunctions perplex our collective incompetence.]
    [Brittle frames snap and decay.]
    [And spectacular miracles still only delay.]

Or the covetous displaced:
    [Venomous kisses breaking our fragile hearts.]
    [Microscopic gifts: the recipient's curse.]
    [Salivating mouths long to be near.]

Or the caretaker's hourglass:
    [Teetering on the edge of the shelf.]
    [Concealing sands, distracting our gaze.]
    [Grainy innards gathered to fall.]

We march… until we don't.

NEVER MIND

Don't give it up…

To political pundits—
with sponsors and greed.
Bias and ratings—
their only real creed.

Prejudiced prophets.
Manipulation with hate.
Scheming to draw,
lines that separate.

Don't give it up…

To advisory peers—
who all know you better.
Even when they are docile,
caring and tender.

They've loved you for years,
so they lend you an ear.
But they're just like the rest:
motivated by fear

Don't give it up…

To shepherds in black
(claiming oneness with God).
They're lost in the world,
painting wishful beyonds.

Faux benevolence wrapped
in whimsical lessons.
Cold dogmatic keys
to unlock what they've destined.

Don't give it up…

To the king of the hill—
with his army and guns.
Selling your daughters
and killing your sons.

Holding lives in balance,
He's the law of the land.
He's the conquesting fool.
He's the ground where they stand.

Don't give it up…

To scholars with books,
degrees and awards.
Corrupted by lies
they still can't afford.

Propaganda and spite—
the brainwasher's guide.
With susceptible youth,
their egos preside.

Don't give it up…

To factionist tribes—
never fully to these.
They will infect,
like a deadly disease.

Instead, trust in love
and a star that won't die.
Yes: love is the way
for all of mankind.

THE GHOST MAKER

And I became her—the one who had eluded me all these years.
    The one with whom I could find no reason.
    The Vacillator.

And I absorbed her—the one absorbed in herself.
    The one possessed from beyond.
    The Volatile.

And I pitied her—the one who had cast me out.
    The one who slit my throat.
    The Monarch.

And I accepted her—the one who can't reciprocate.
    The one who craves chaos.
    The Puppet Master.

And I reject her—the one without heart.
    The one who loathes her duty.
    The Ghost Maker.

DISPASSION

He's a song without passion—
strummed with logic and insight.
Steady. Reasonable. Boring.

He's a kiss without feeling—
placed with obligation and habit.
Muscle memories guiding his apathy.

He's a flame without kindling—
burning without a base on a windy hill.
Fleeting. Dying. Predictable.

He's the man without purpose—
scraping by with fast-fading dreams.
Robotic. Empty. Deluded.

He's the poem you don't get—
scattered words without significance.
Emotionless. Esoteric. Useless.

CHANGED

Water to wine:

Red castoff splatter,
Smeared on drawn shades,
Above her cramped cushiony crate,
Where my debaucherous vampire sleeps.

Genteel to crass:

A trampled young lamb.
Broken legs to support the mob's gossip.
Slaughtered below countless identical Hydes,
Where my doting doctor once stood.

Chaste to embraced:

Ascending grime on the stairs.
Muddy tracks from outside
Lead to the stalked, red-robed tribute,
Where my carnal lycanthrope smiles.

Pupil to truant:

Books in a dumpster—
Obscured from her view,
In the forgotten narrow alley,
Where my succubus discarded the cure.

Like clear skies to thunder.
Transformed, now, I wonder,
"Why has she left me estranged?"

I think and I ponder:
"Why didn't I stop her?"
Then I realized 'twas I who had changed.

"I AGREE"

You were a word—a name.
Faceless and hollow,
no need to follow.
'Til she brought you…
and everything changed.

You were personified—a curious guest.
Perched on the step,
my focus now wrecked.
'Til you saw me…
and ignited my quest.

You were a number—a digital list.
Dialed sometimes,
reserved space in my mind.
'Til I swung…
and you told me I missed.

You were unattainable—a disease with no cure.
Despondent and weary,
No response to my query.
'Til I kissed you…
and let my passion endure.

You were romanced fruition—a "Beauty" with me.
A rose in your car,
anticipating afar
'Til you wrote me
and said "I agree."

DIVIDE AND DEVOUR

Predators in designer suits.
Plastic smiles and thirsty for blood.
Yours. Mine. Ours.

Corralling and dividing our mass.
Nipping our hooves, while the herd blames itself:
Pharisees. Comrades. And me.

Crosses, hammers and sickles—
Refurbished weapons from the lions who hunt us.
Misunderstood. Misused. And misdirected.

Pouncing felines, fat from our flesh.
Parasitical drive so they swipe at our backs.
Silvery eyes. Golden teeth. And deadly green claws.

Dodging right. Veering left. We scatter.
My isolation—a weakness exploited though pride.
I'm alone. And surrounded. To prey.

Surprisingly nimble—these decorative killers.
Hot breath on my neck, as my jugular tears.
Distracted cattle reforming. Gorging puppeteers feasting. And you.

LEMON

I stand on the precipice of the abyss
(a chasm of pure darkness enveloping the world).

It has consumed sky and Earth alike.
Below my feet: a solitary patch of ground.

I cannot go back.
Gone is the mountain path I climbed to get here.

I cannot go forward.
A step in any direction to begin my final plunge.

My body shakes like a failing engine,
humming loudly as the resounding emptiness pours into me.

I gasp and gag, as it wraps 'round my choking lungs.
It's inside of me—searching for my soul.

To move is to die.
To stay still would be worse.

Yet I stare out into the cruel and abounding fate I've wrought for myself.
Manifested darkness obscuring all but my mind.

And I convulse as the world tightens around me—squeezing me
    like a vice.
My life is a dried out lemon (a hollow and useless husk).

And the terror of it all keeps me trembling in place,
for I know:

There's nowhere else to go…
There's nowhere else to go…

COMPASS

This compass: "defective."
That's what I received.
Thought: "better perspective,"
but I was deceived.

To journey like this,
with an instrument, faulty.
Like walking through mist,
as it blinds and assaults me.

Still… time to embark
(or maybe not quite).
Avoiding the dark
but longing for night.

Day could be better
(less danger in light).
A place to surrender?
Or maybe to fight…

I wonder and walk
'til the path finally splits.
I stop there and balk,
at the end of my wits.

What says my compass?
It lends me no answers.
Instead, it's a rumpus
of stressed, mental clatter.

This road is perfect.
That one is broken.
"Still, it might work,"
(in my mind, where it's spoken).

"The road less-traveled."
I've decided at last.
But it all comes unraveled,
when I recall the past.

Before I left home,
I packed and prepared
but now I'm alone
and my thoughts are impaired.

Approaching an orchard,
my mind turns to food.
Still, though, it's tortured
and far from improved.

This fruit might be rotten.
I'll leave it alone.
But I haven't forgotten
my stomach's deep groan.

It growls like the beast
whose domain I had entered.
I dealt him defeat,
though I might have surrendered.

He was covered in blood—
his victims', I'm sure.
Unless it was mud
and his heart was still pure.

In that case, I think:
I chose incorrect.
Like a pen with dry ink
(its lackluster effect).

Should I have run?
Maybe eaten the fruit?
Should I have come
on this exact route?

What says my compass?
It lends me no answers.
Instead, it's a rumpus
of stressed, mental clatter.

Daylight or night?
So many decisions.
Fighting or flight?
(with all my revisions).

What should I have packed?
My choice: wrong or right?
Those apples: to snack?
When's my respite?

My compass points one way
but then to another.
I'm filled with dismay.
It shrouds like a cover.

These corroded gears
(from time's toxic touch).
Too many dark years.
The internals are mush.

So I sit in the dirt,
where I postulate
on why it's inert
and I vacillate.

THE SEVENTH

A mansion for one. Opulent, spacious and vacant. The "echo-maker." Pristine and unsettled. Exclusive but common enough. "Such wondrous potential:" repeated gibberish he can't seem to mute.

But it's all his. His dwelling since birth. Free, uninhibited and alone. Always alone. Massive servants doting on his every whim will find no quarter. Yet they indulge. The id. Always the id. Only the id. Only him. From his throne, his garbled, high-pitched commands bounce off empty halls and beckon helpless giants. Their curse. Their blessing. Their regret. Their sentence.

Then… a squatter. A reluctant invader. Conscripted and bitter. Adolescent and pock-marked. Reclusive and unsure. The "Floor-Watcher." Skulking, nervous and silent. He finds a room and locks the door. His secret refuge. The newest tenant.

Until the new king. On silver-dollar-sized, four-wheeled self-propulsion, he arrives. The green-haired revivalist. Duct-tape wrapped around a dirty, ripped sneaker. It breaches the door. Cowering children tremble with admiration, while their savior usurps the throne.

Their halls shrink and their world seems small. Forgotten, they watch from the shadows. They peek through keyholes, while loud music clings to cancerous clouds. The anarchist's lonely rule: obnoxious and rude. Defiant and crass. An angsty romantic, caked in an invisible, exclusionary filth.

Then the rest. First student, then drunk, then peddler arrive. The mansion has shrunk. Cramped. Nowhere to think. Nowhere to "be." A jumbled and confusing mess. They're a noisy triad (fraternizing inmates). Their home: neglected and unkempt. The giants: long gone.

The drunk, the student, the peddler, the punker, the adolescent, the kid. Baggage piled in every room. Hoarders. Squalor, laced with confusion and apathy. Disarray and dismay. 'Til that knock on the half-hanging door. He's there. He's always there. So I open it…

BREATHING FREELY

I am the transient spire atop their debauched temple.
(where they affix these tarnished blocks of life to their moldy,
    mossy shingles).

I am the observant gargoyle, perched on high, flicking flames at the
    boisterous rabble below.
(where they dodge my waning magic and try goading me into
    casting another singeing volley).

I am the rising heat, surrounded by multi-colored, artistic explosions
    igniting the vacant skyline.
(where a myriad of tiny fireballs sizzle into an empty haze, above
    the bustle of misguided freedom).

I am the compromised ventilation of a terminal city; my flue spews
    my infection into the night.
(where it cascades down and is drawn into the lungs of the
    oblivious dreamers).

I am the lion on the mountain—my pride captured by jackals
    patrolling a treacherous sidewalk.
(where they gather to watch my breath, on this clear, muggy night).

I am the flaming archer stationed on the tower, alongside a plethora
    of burning munitions.
(where my compatriots offer more deadly, fiery projectiles for my
    empty, pocket-sized quiver).

I am the pinnacle of enslavement—the prisoner locked high atop a
    mighty fort.
(where I abandon my leisurely suicide, onto the inflammable
    concrete below).

I am the sentient statue whose outstretched fingers curl into a fist
    and repel the wild fowl.
(where I embody the date and signal a new freedom of my own design).

I am the target situated above the tree-line.
(where their jeers harden my resolve and soften the raised atmosphere).

I am the steamy, melted remnants of an oppressive regime, oozing
    down through shoddy rafters.
(where I'll dissolve wooden barricades and then drip onto the ground
    below).

I am the quickly-cooling, molten puddle—poured out, onto a
    neglected, shabby street.
(where, over time, my convictions solidify and I find myself able to
    breathe once more).

THIRTY SECONDS

Under the warm, July sun, an icy frigid chill.
From another reality, it slinks down his back.

It's a startling shiver, like frozen acupuncture needles—
from behind his ears, to the radiant wooden slats on which he sits.

A familiar signal. An ominous, impending dread,
from an intrusive gateway he cannot manage.

(Thirty Seconds)

The astral stopwatch is interminably engaged,
from a reflected, one-way road on the precipice of perception.

Innumerable obelisks (foreign yet painfully familiar) are manifesting,
from above his head, where their encircling shadows deny the sun.

No words or gestures, yet their castigations commence,
from internalized ideas their master excavated.

We thought them safely mired… secluded… entombed,
from within the dammed, glistening quagmire of his unexplored soul.

They admonish, critique, accuse and expose,
from the swirling, cyclonic structures forming above his head.

Closer…
Closer…

Closer…
They're walling his crypt.

(Fifteen Seconds)

Spasms, and intermittent seizures in the frigid July heat,
from under their shadows, where the sun cannot spread.

A moistened brow, atrophied legs and darkening eyes.
From their mirrored influence, he cannot escape.

Better to die standing so his slouched back inches upward, against
    warm, grating brick.
From that stance, his wobbly legs await the squad's lead.

Closer…
Closer…
Closer…
The light is faint.

(Ten)

Strangers watch him try and peer beyond the nothing.

(Nine)

They attack with hushed whispers and curious eyes…

(Eight)

"You're not good enough!"

(Seven)

"You're going to fail!"

(Six)

"Loveless!"

(Five)

Deadly gas pours into the makeshift chamber.

(Four)

No room left. He cannot breathe.

(Three)

The inevitable beckons.

(Two)

A solitary crack of light against the nebulous, abounding abyss.

(One)

A LUMINOUS PARASITE

It's got me again.
A luminous parasite in all its superficial splendor
(hypnotizing and draining my essence).

It insists.
Burdening me, like a petulant child assigned to my care.
Blade to my throat, I enrolled in my fate.

It bleeds me.
Its voracious appetite, consuming electrified sand from my vault.
With constant proposals, amendments and feedings, I am consumed.

It's growing.
Heavier every day but always the same weight.
Its innards evolving its collective, predatory nature.

It persists.
Never quiet for long.
Slicing its vocal cords yields no difference.

It's "survival."
Birds on the back of a bison; remoras attached to the shark; "You
    need it!"
Expertly shrouding parasitical intent under a symbiotic guise.

It's evolving.
Newer, sleeker, adaptable and deadly (like The Hydra).
Severing its own heads to make way for fresher ones.

It's a disease.
The drug for which there is no rehab; the itch I cannot scratch.
Always absorbing, always mutating, always spreading its infection.

It's a calling.
Monopolizing existence with useless propositions and
   thinly-veiled promises
(like the poorly-cast ring I've reluctantly taken). It's got me again.

A COMFORTABLE COMPROMISE

Novocained assurance.
They lend it in spades.
It's a common occurrence
and a simplistic trade.

For a third of your life,
Just adapt their routine.
Abandon all strife.
Accept their guarantee.

But it's not without cost.
No; a soul isn't cheap.
No return of what's lost,
when they keep you asleep.

Where they broadcast their dreams.
Where they grow all their kingdoms.
Where you'll join in their schemes
and become their next victim.

Banal, stuffed and numb—
it's the life they would offer.
Enticing to some,
(to be captured and smothered).

Or forge your own plans—
though you might not succeed.
It's a dangerous dance,
yet fulfilling and free.

Their perks or your voice?
It's their dream or yours.
I've made my own choice,
and my voice yet endures.

NOTE FROM THE AUTHOR

Dear Reader,

If you enjoyed *The Esoterian: Ramblings of a Madman*, please consider leaving a review on Amazon, Goodreads or on any one of your favorite online book sellers.

In most cases, reviews are the lifeblood of an author's career so, even if yours is only a few words, it would still help me immensely.

Thank you in advance and, if you're so inclined, please also feel free to connect with me online:

Website: www.ehmbeeway.com
Instagram: @ehmbee_way
Facebook: Ehmbee Way
YouTube: @ehmbeeway
Tiktok: @ehmbee_way

All the best,

Ehmbee

ABOUT THE AUTHOR

Ehmbee Way is a former corporate success who earned his undergraduate degree in the field of education. In early 2023, he published his first full-length novel, Compunction—a suspenseful, character-driven, upmarket fiction, centered around a redemptive theme. In his spare time, he enjoys music, podcasts, reading,  gaming and riding his motorcycle. He also considers himself to be a spiritual man, an avid dog lover and a recovered alcoholic.